C000233543

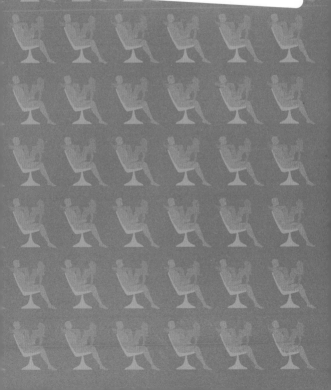

KAMA SUTRA
SEX TIPS

THIS IS A CARLTON BOOK

Text and design copyright © Carlton Books
Limited 2008

This edition published by
Carlton Books Limited
20 Mortimer Street
London W1T 3JW

ISBN 978 1 84732 212 8

Printed and bound in China

Senior Executive Editor: Lisa Dyer
Senior Art Editor: Gülen Shevki-Taylor
Design: Zoë Dissell
Production: Kate Pimm

KAMA SUTRA
SEX TIPS

LISA SWEET

CARLTON
BOOKS

introduction

If you think the Kama Sutra is just about boosting your bedroom antics, think again. Sure, it's chock-a-block full of exotic passion positions designed to lift you out of missionary monotony, but it's also about living the life erotic: sensually, spiritually and psychologically (*Kamashastra* means 'treatise on sexual pleasure'). According to the ancient text, women are as sexual as men, and (our personal favourite) men should work towards providing women with erotic pleasure, including orgasms. In other words, *Sex and the City* around 300 AD.

Even if you're not interested in
converting to a Kama lifestyle, you can
still take up some swift techniques that
will help you last longer, orgasm harder
and get bathing-suit curves. Okay, so you
probably won't get the insta-curves, but you'll
burn up your bedroom every time.

Sound good? Then read on for a totally modern round-
up to the most titillating tips from the original book on
love. Whether you already have a partner to play with
or you're swinging solo, you'll crank the temperature
from between your ears to between your legs – with
a few sultry stops in between!

Be forewarned. You're about to embark
on a trip towards total
out-of-body
enlightenment.

Boost Your Spirits

1

'...pleasures, being as
necessary for the existence and
wellbeing of the body as food,
are consequently equally required...'

Sex, the Kama Sutra way, has far more going on
than two naked bodies playing a hot and heavy version
of mattress mambo before they conk out. The best
kind of carnal connection begins *outside* the bedroom with
shared intimate habits tuning in to your sexual spirit
to create more passion in your life and a deeper
bond with your lover.

So, before you start stroking, get smokin' by channelling
your sexual energy. Body-blistering results guaranteed!

Mental Twists

Here are ten simple steps for slipping into a sexy state of mind. You'll discover a side to lovemaking that you never thought possible.

1

✳ **Know your love.** There are four oh-so-lusty ways to connect with your partner in passion:

Desire it: The more you want it, the more you think and obsess about it.

Believe it: The more you know you are desired, the stronger the link between you and the higher the temperature in bed.

Keep it up: The more you get off with each other, the more you'll want to get it on with each other.

Show it: The more PDAs you give, the higher you amp your PPQ (Partner Passion Quotient).

2

✳ **Shake your booty.** Mojo is one of the sexiest accessories you can have in bed – not only does it make you feel fabulous but it also boosts your amour adrenalin, making you more inclined to give new moves a go. This isn't about performance – it's about the satisfaction and pleasure you get simply being in each other's aura. Fortunately, confidence is one of those fake-it-till-you-make-it things – the more you pretend you have it, the more you feel like you have it, and ergo – the more you have it.

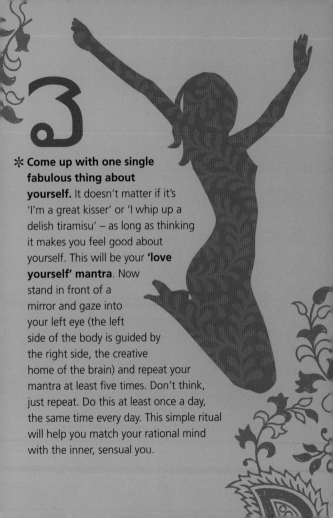

3

✷ **Come up with one single fabulous thing about yourself.** It doesn't matter if it's 'I'm a great kisser' or 'I whip up a delish tiramisu' – as long as thinking it makes you feel good about yourself. This will be your **'love yourself' mantra**. Now stand in front of a mirror and gaze into your left eye (the left side of the body is guided by the right side, the creative home of the brain) and repeat your mantra at least five times. Don't think, just repeat. Do this at least once a day, the same time every day. This simple ritual will help you match your rational mind with the inner, sensual you.

Get into the groove. Ritual transforms the everyday into the sacred. It could be as elaborate as scattering rose petals on your duvet every night or as simple as IMing 'I <3 U' the same time every day. **Five instant ways to connect:**

✳ Set up a daily love shrine by putting two small heart pillows on your bed.
✳ Wake with a hug and a kiss.
✳ After you make your bed, mist the sheet with your perfume so it holds your scent.
✳ Light a fragrant candle every night once you are home.
✳ End the night with your song.

5 Get hands-on even when you're not hoping to get it on. Kiss for no reason, swap foot rubs just because, play finger games every chance you get… By physically connecting in small ways as much as possible, you'll stay on **simmer for hotter action later on**. And you'll still feel close on those (unavoidable) nights when you're too beat to do more.

6 Form a **mutual admiration society**, no other members allowed. Take delight in each other's company, cherishing your time together vertically as well as horizontally. Play a game, dance, cook a meal together or simply turn off the television, sit and hold hands and swap childhood stories. Getting to know your lover can be an amazing turn-on.

7 The **art of singing** and playing music have an important role in lovemaking. According to the KS, when 'word becomes too much for expression, the romantic longing of crooning and strumming comes'. Those with no musical talent can do air guitar or karaoke, though it may not have quite the same erotic effect.

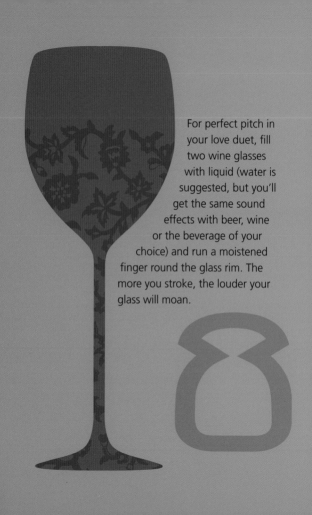

For perfect pitch in your love duet, fill two wine glasses with liquid (water is suggested, but you'll get the same sound effects with beer, wine or the beverage of your choice) and run a moistened finger round the glass rim. The more you stroke, the louder your glass will moan.

Stimulate your **intellectual fusion** by playing together. Riddles, crossword puzzles, cards and tongue-twisters are all considered fair game in the art of love.

Go for a **transcendental quickie**. For a power surge of connection and love, lie down facing each other, place your right hands on each other's hearts and lock eyes. The longer you hold the pose, the better in step you'll be when you start your racy tango.

Lift the Mood

Take your randy romps to an even higher plane with a few simple shifts in scenery.

Flowers are important in Kama Sutra. They bloom with nature and sensuality. One of the 64 arts is learning to make artificial bouquets to decorate the house (knowledge of weapons, gymnastics and carpentry are also listed). **To make your garden grow:**

* Stack four 15 x 30 cm (6 x 12 in) pieces of colourful tissue paper.
* Fold from the bottom as if making a fan, concertina-style, back and forth in 2.5 cm (1 in) folds.
* Round off the ends by trimming them with scissors.
* Fold a green pipe cleaner in half and twist it around the centre of the tissues.
* Fan out the paper on both sides of the pipe cleaner and, starting with the top tissue, carefully begin pulling up the 'petals'.
* When all the layers have been pulled out, spritz a light mist of perfume on to your flower and place it somewhere it will be seen.

12. Create an ambience in strategic locations around the house where you plan to take action. Try setting out perfumed flowers, scented votive candles or incense (musk, sandalwood and jasmine are particularly ardent aromas) ranged along windowsills, shelves and tables. Drape coloured silks and cloths over your furniture and lower the lighting. The point is to make your space feel like a temple of love.

13 Make sure the room is toasty warm (you'll be naked for a while).

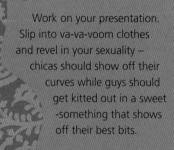

Work on your presentation.
Slip into va-va-voom clothes
and revel in your sexuality –
chicas should show off their
curves while guys should
get kitted out in a sweet
-something that shows
off their best bits.

Put at least
one item
on display that
shouts out your love
– of yourself or a
partner. This might be
a holiday photo, a special
knick-knack or even a pebble
or some other memento of
a happy time.

Secret Sex Spots

Great sex isn't just about technique, it's about being fully absorbed in the experience with all of your being. Try these sensational spa moments at home.

With these sizzling to-do's for cleaning up your act, you'll both be primed for a down-and-dirty divine time!

✷ Carefully shave his face. Leave a moustache – it's considered to have he-man qualities (plus it'll **tickle those hard-to-reach places** under your personal boudoir).

✷ Transform your daily bath from a basic wash into a **steamy sexploit**. Turn off your phone, TV and the lights. Now's a great time to use flickering (and flattering) candlelight. Put on a softly romantic CD, stack some lush towels and place a flower in a vase where you can focus on its beauty. Soak and meditate. Nurture yourself as much as possible.

✳ Turn up the water temperature by including your partner in the tub. Take time to **rub-a-dub-dub** each other with loving care. Water relaxes the body and is a symbol of balanced sexuality. Use therapeutic rubs and luxurious scrubs and oils to get each other squeaky clean, silky soft and gloriously uninhibited. Finish off by using a cup to pour warm water over each other's back, neck and chest, over and over and – sigh – over again.

✳ Take turns in giving each other a slo-mo shampoo. The scalp is tingling with **touch-me-now nerves**. At the same time you're drawing your bath, fill the sink with hot water and a few drops of essential oil, then submerge a towel in the mixture. Sit in the tub – whoever is hairstylist for the day sits at the back so they can drizzle a generous helping of shampoo (the extra lather will feel lush) all over their lover's hair. They should then interlace their fingers and place their hands on top of the recipient's head, gently pressing and rubbing the base of their palms against the scalp. Work a super-sudsy froth towards the back of the head, up towards the top and over to the forehead. Spend a little time kneading the earlobes (a much-overlooked hot zone). Fill a pitcher with clean, warm water, gently tilt their head back and rinse out the shampoo. Since this step is overcharged with sensuality, don't be surprised at the groans and moans.

The colour of your teeth, clothes, nails, hair and body can make you literally loopy with sensuality. **Here's how to get a hue:**

✱ Brush with a whitening toothpaste. Cinnamon-flavoured will stir his blood.

✱ Henna yourself beautiful by adding shades of red to your hair or staining your skin with exotic patterns.

✱ Body art should be sexy but it can also be tasty. The Kama Sutra Lover's Paintbox (a jar of chocolate mousse and a soft paintbrush, available from most sex shops) will make a lovemaster out of anyone.

✱ Tattooing is considered one of the vital arts but you may not want to make your love quite so permanent. Instead, spend the evening sticking on temporary tats or body jewels.

✱ Make it a mani-pedi night. Candy pink, deep purple and ruby red are all considered tantalizing tints.

17

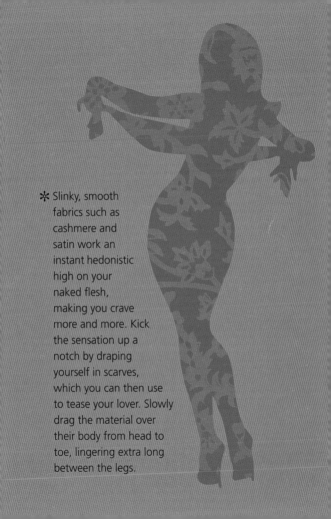

✳ Slinky, smooth fabrics such as cashmere and satin work an instant hedonistic high on your naked flesh, making you crave more and more. Kick the sensation up a notch by draping yourself in scarves, which you can then use to tease your lover. Slowly drag the material over their body from head to toe, lingering extra long between the legs.

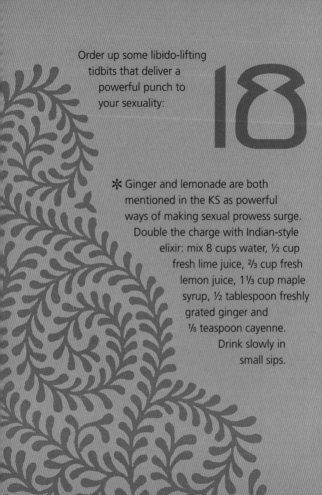

Order up some libido-lifting tidbits that deliver a powerful punch to your sexuality:

18

✳ Ginger and lemonade are both mentioned in the KS as powerful ways of making sexual prowess surge. Double the charge with Indian-style elixir: mix 8 cups water, ½ cup fresh lime juice, ⅔ cup fresh lemon juice, 1⅓ cup maple syrup, ½ tablespoon freshly grated ginger and ⅛ teaspoon cayenne. Drink slowly in small sips.

✷ Drinking milk, mixed with sugar and the boiled testicle of a ram or a goat, is supposed to work your wham-bam. Luckily, the wonder herb Ashwagandha seems to have the same effect and is more readily available as a tea from any Ayurvedic practitioner.

✷ If a man mixes raw rice with eggs (the KS suggests sparrow eggs but you can substitute ordinary eggs), boils it in milk, adds ghee and honey and drinks as much of it as he can, he will be transformed into a super-stud with amazing long-lasting powers.

✷ His penis will be enlarged if he eats pomegranate seeds. The cortisone-like chemicals in the fruit stimulate the adrenal gland, where adrenaline is born.

✷ Forget loading her up with beer. A far cheaper, more seductive way to start her motor is to embrace her with his left arm while holding a cup of mango juice for her to drink. Afterwards, he should kiss her mouth softly and gracefully without making a sound.

Suck It Up

Breathing deeply
brings you in touch
with your body
instead of your mind.
Read on to Tip 23
to improve your
air supply.

On your own: Sit and
place your hands just
below your belly button. Inhale
deeply. Breathe deeply through the nose, so that
the belly pushes out. Exhale until your belly
contracts back to the spine. Repeat nine times.

Before you even think about sex, sit on the bed or floor facing your partner (on his lap), close your eyes and begin swaying as if you're in a rocker. Move forwards as you inhale, tightening your PC muscle (the pelvic floor muscle you use to control your flow of pee) at the same time. Then exhale and release as you rock back.

21

A mid-play breath check: Keep in touch during foreplay – his right hand goes on her heart, her right hand is placed on his heart; her left hand covers his right, his left covers her right. Begin breathing in unison while gazing into each other's eyes. Hold until one of you blinks or laughs.

22

In the final moment: A lot of people tighten up when they get close to climaxing, but try exhaling at the crucial moment and you'll spread the joy throughout your body.

23

Anytime: Cuddle together in the traditional 'spoons' position, curved together with your arms around each other. Pay attention to the rhythm of your partner's breathing and gradually start to synchronize your ins and outs. Soon you'll be so attuned to each other's puffs that you'll become an extension of each other.

Must-have Pleasure Tools

These essential lust-tested props will harmonize the mind and body to work as one.

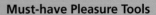

Boost his ego. After sex, rub his *lingam* (aka penis) with almond oil until it begins to swell. Slip on a scrunchie hair accessory and send him to bed on his tummy. The next morning, stroke his stoke with a cool mint ointment. Have more sex that night and repeat the oil/ scrunchie/sleep combo. Keep it up and in a few days, his 'bad boy' will be bigger and better than ever.

25

Put your senses on high alert by keeping a blindfold nearby.

26

Invest in cheat sheets. Karma Sheetras (www.kamasheetra.com) guide you Twister-style through the basic positions.

27

You'll need some motion lotion to kama-sutrize your love life. Lube boosts below-the-belt sensation and allows him to thrust longer and harder without giving her pain. Grease up with a product that doubles up as a massage oil such as K-Y Touch Massage 2-in-1 Warming (www.ky.com), ID Velvet Lubricating Liquid (www.idlube.com) and Kama Sutra Love Liquid (kamasutra.com).

Put a buzz in your play with a sprinkling of honey dust. Mix 1 cup arrowroot powder with 3 tablespoons honey powder and then spatter it on with a feather duster. Store in an airtight container.

28

29

The KS was one of the first texts to mention a penis extender, suggesting that they can be crafted from wood, leather, buffalo horn, copper, silver, ivory or gold. Much easier is to get Curve, a silicone dildo shaped for pleasure (www.bedtimeheaven.co.uk). Its bumps and lumps hit all the right spots while the curved handle (get it?) makes it easy to rock back and forth, so you find just the right angle for maximum enjoyment. Use it as a lover's little helper when he needs to stop and recharge his batteries.

2
Moan-athon

'Women are like flowers and
need to be enticed very tenderly.'

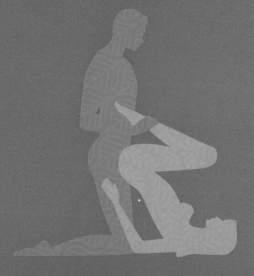

To focus on the full sexual journey, take the slow road to the ecstasy ramp. The idea is to stay just below your boiling limit for as long as possible, paying attention to every neglected nook and cranny. This gives you time to merge your bodies' rhythms, senses and desires. What could be sexier than that?

These Omigod kiss-and-touch techniques will help you build on your bond. Put any or all of these moves together in any order, depending on your mood, and the need to cool or heat things up a little.

30 Smooch It Up

Kissing is as intimate a deed as the actual act of sex itself. Here's how to make mouth magic:

- Get the seduction going with a **Bent Kiss** – your heads angle towards each other and your lips connect very, very gently.
- Turn on by kissing **Turned-style**. Reach out and while cradling your lover's chin, turn their face up towards you.
- For an oh-so-hot smooch, give it to him straight on – lock lips without touching any other part of his body.
- Get a tingly sensation by giving him a **Clasping Kiss**. Take both his lips between your own and nibble gently. (In the KS, a woman only bestows this kiss on a man with no moustache – perhaps because the hairs would get caught in her mouth.)
- Make him drool with a **Greatly Pressed Kiss**. Take hold of the lower lip between two fingers and, after caressing it with your tongue, strongly press your lips against it. Crank things up a notch by licking the rim of each other's lips and get your whole body into the act of making out by grabbing his butt while you grind against him.
- For a passionate, gotta-have-it-now lip lock, do the **Fight with Your Tongues**. Tease him by tracing the outside of his lips with your tongue, gently tugging his bottom lip with your teeth, and lightly biting his tongue whenever it's in your mouth.

31

Sweeten your kisses by sucking each other's lips as you concentrate on breathing in tandem.

32

Plant light kisses all over his face while he's asleep. Known as the 'kiss that kindles love', it's KS-lingo for saying, 'Let's get it on'.

33

Make your smooches feel like oral sex by tugging on his tongue. Because the tongue muscle is connected to the throat, you actually end up stimulating the muscles in his neck and chest with this move – so one kiss will work up his whole torso.

34

Go public with your love on the quiet. When you're out in the world, present your finger (when you're standing) or toe (if you're sitting) for him to feast upon.

Instead of giving him the usual peck when you meet-and-greet, slay him with a full-on wet and slobbery kiss.

35

Pretend to be nodding off when he comes home so that he can bestow some 'kiss that awakens' on you. Warning: Accepting these love tokens are a promise of still more lusty delights.

36

Kisses are not
a lips-only affair.
Other hot spots
to nuzzle include
the forehead,
eyelids, cheeks,
throat, breasts,
thighs, arms and
belly button.

37

Make a bet:
Whoever catches
the other's lower
lips between their
teeth first wins.
(You decide stakes.)

38

Bite Me

The Kama Sutra says if you can kiss it, you can bite it (the only exceptions are the upper lip, the inside of the mouth and the eyes).

While there are hundreds of ways to nibble each other, these love bites are guaranteed to inspire gotta-have-it-now sensations. But one hint before you start: this isn't about vampire draw-blood chomps; rather, you gently catch your lover's tender skin between your teeth and lips – aka, your 'coral and jewel'. Think of sthem as love tokens:

* Gently nip with your teeth, leaving behind a **Hidden Bite** of slight redness.
* Suck as you bite to create a **Swollen Bite** of bliss.
* Make a **Line of Points** by squeezing the flesh with all your teeth.

Keep things sensual by limiting your feast to the throat, breasts, armpits and thighs.

Some bites are best saved for when you're in Ooh! Ah! Ooh! mode:

✴ Making a **Broken Cloud** with marks in an uneven circle around the twins (breasts).
✴ Constantly biting to create the **Biting of the Boar** – rows of marks on the breasts and shoulders.

শ্রী

Whatever he does
to you, do back.

Don't just bite and
leave – gently blow on
the area afterwards to
create a steamy heat.

Touch Me
Get ready to rub each
other up the right way.

Here are the six
different kinds of soul-
satisfying embraces
every hot-blooded
lover should master:

* Keep things simmering with a **Touching Embrace**. Giving each other soft, unexpected strokes throughout the day can be very erotic, reminding your partner that you are still there, and of what is to come.
* Sneak up behind him and push your breasts against him, giving him every opportunity to reach up and twiddle your dials with a **Piercing Embrace**.
* The next time you're walking together, push your love to a higher plane by melding your bodies together in a **Pressing Embrace**.
* Cling like a vine to your man by tightly hugging him so closely that your arms and thighs encircle and rub against each other in a **Twining of the Creeper**. Pump up the love vibe by purring 'sut sut' in his ear.
* Offer up a **Milk-and-Water Embrace** with a lap dance that will have him giving you a standing Oh-vation.
* Embrace your lover's thighs by catching their legs between yours and squeezing them in small passion pulses.

Seek out new spots. If your usual routine is to caress their neck, then their bottom and to move on over to their package, work on the shoulders, temples and the backs of the thighs. Switching your MO keeps you awake to the moment.

45

46

Gun your motors by moving in ultra-slow motion.

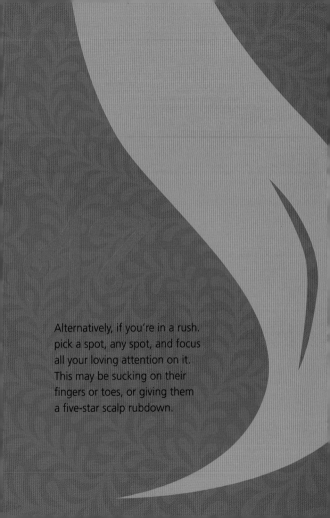

Alternatively, if you're in a rush.
pick a spot, any spot, and focus
all your loving attention on it.
This may be sucking on their
fingers or toes, or giving them
a five-star scalp rubdown.

Keep an eye on each other. The more you can maintain your gaze during foreplay, the greater in tune you will be with each other's desires (see Tip 21 for how to gaze eye-to-eye, sutra-style).

Do the hokey-pokey with his *lingam* and her *yoni* (vagina): Hold the *lingam* in the right hand and turn it around her *yoni*. Now pierce just the upper part of his *lingam* into the *yoni*. Finally, rub, press and tap – that's what it's all about.

Slaps and Tickles

A little gentle pain can be oh-yes sensational, snapping both of you back into the moment. But be sure not to kill the mood with over-zealous sexual aggression.

With him prone, climb aboard facing his feet so you can focus all of your sweet energy on those often-skipped ultra-sensitive nerves in his lower body. Work a generous amount of lube into your palms (grease refuels at Tip 27) and lightly slap and tickle the entire area. Follow up with some long, sensuous strokes to make him squirm with pleasure. When he's ready to explode, spank him silly, slipsliding your hands ever-so-close to his love triangle.

50

51

Press *jaghanas* (sounds better than 'bellies') while languorously scratching each other's backs with long, sweeping, sensuous moves.

52.

Squeeze his nipples
between your own
rosebuds.

53

Get intense, down-and-dirty, rough and raw – bite, scratch, squeeze, rub, pinch, poke… It's furious foreplay with all the messy trimmings. Don't turn down the volume. Moan, coo, sigh, hiss, cry, groan, shriek and shout for all you're worth!

Give a jolt during sex by gently nipping your partner's shoulders or an earlobe.

54

Bend your
**naughty
sweetheart**
over your
knee and
paddle their
bare bottom with
a wooden spoon.

55

Slowly **trace figure-of-eights** as you run your nails down his inner thigh, along his armpit, over his throat, across his nipples, and along the belly, gradually increasing the pressure.

56

57

Gently stroke his skin with your nails so that the hair stands on end.

58

If your lover is going on a journey, make a **Token of Remembrance** on their thighs or chest by pressing your nails into the skin to create three or four close lines.

Blow Your Mind

3

'Stirring the root of her thighs,
which her own hands
are gripping and holding widely apart,
your fluted tongue drinks
at her sacred spring.'

All oral sex is not created equally. The difference between an okay trip Down South and a Kama Sutra Mouth Congress sure to electrify your bedroom bond is to work a bunch of sensations into the act – using your lips, your tongue, your teeth, your hands and even your body in combo of moves known as Lovemaking of the Crow is sure to make you both caw with delight.

So don't be afraid to vary the pressure, the caress or even the position mid-lick. As a bonus, this gives you the perfect excuse to switch gears whenever you get tired.

Giving Lip Service
Double your pleasure with
these below-the-belt tricks.

A great blow-job is not all mouth, all of the time. Here's
how to make beautiful music on his organ. This series
of fresh **Crow techniques** will have him flying in nine
easy steps. Make it even more of a thrill by changing
the pace and pressure as you play.

* Warm him up with *nimitta*: Hold his goodies firmly
  in your hand, making an 'O' with your lips around its
  tip. Move your head in small circles.
* Once you're feeling relaxed and comfy and he's
  starting to squirm, move on to **Nominal Congress**.
  Start working your lips and tongue around the
  head of his *lingam*.
* Make him wriggle by **Biting the Sides**. Grasp
  the head of his *lingam* in your hand and
  gently caress one side of his shaft, then
  the other, with your lips and tongue.

* When he's gasping for air, move on to the **Outer Pincers**. Less painful than it sounds, you take the head of his *lingam* gently between your parted lips and press sucking kisses tenderly against it. Use your fingers to very gently pull at the soft skin of the shaft. Think the in-and-out motion and you've got it.

* Switch to **Inner Pincers** and work him into a lather. Slide his whole head into your mouth, pressing the shaft between your lips, holding and pulling away, holding and pulling away.

* Holding him in your hand, use your lips and tongue to perform ***chumbitaka***. Less complicated than it sounds, you kiss and rub his package from head to toe. Rinse with your mouth and repeat.

* Now rub all over with your tongue and make a wish. Called ***parimshtaka***, you use your tongue to flick him all over before poking it at the mega-sensitive glans at the tip. If he cries out your name, you hit bull's-eye.

* Time to **Suck the Mango**. Take him halfway back inside your mouth and suck hard, as if you 'were stripping clean a mango stone'.

* The previous step will probably make him combust. When he starts to boil over, **Swallow Whole** by sucking all of him up in your mouth.

60

With these brilliant mouth moves, he'll make you flap in **Crow**. He can mix and match according to your lusty needs.

✻ He starts with a **Quivering Kiss**, delicately pinching the swollen lips of your petals together and kissing them in the same way as he'd smooch the lower lip on your mouth.

✻ Now that you're beginning to bloom, he **Circles the Tongue** by gently nuzzling his way inside of your *yoni* with his nose, lips and chin in small spirals. You might want him to shave first!

✻ The **Tongue Massage** will get your nectar flowing. He runs his tongue slowly but firmly back and forth across your love bud before plunging it deeply into your *yoni*, massaging its walls.

✻ Next he performs *cushita* by cupping your bottom and working just the tip of his tongue to probe your belly button before slithering down to your *yoni* and sucking hard.

✻ Using your hands, open out your thighs to give him as much working room as possible for **Stirring Your Yoni** (lapping up all your love water).

✻ Sucking hard is as digit curling as it sounds. He brings your feet to his shoulders, grasps your waist and combines the **Tongue Massage with** *cushita* to blissfully finish you off.

Lie side-by-side, head-to-groin. Now do everything listed in Tips 59 and 60.

61

*'Full of desire, saying sweet words,
approach her with your body stiff as a pole
and drive straight forward
to pierce her lotus and join your limbs.'*

Trying out new sex moves adds a touch of zest
and zing to your play – but not if you crash and
burn. There are literally hundreds of possible pleasure
positions in the Kama Sutra (529, to be precise), so
read on for titillating twists on the classic four anyone-
can-do poses: Missionary, Woman on Top, Rear Entry
and Side by Side.

None require acrobatics or props but all will bond you
spiritually as well as physically. Oh, and they'll also propel
you both into a fiery frenzy. Now that's spirited sex.

Size Things Up
Get in sync.

62.

For the sauciest union,
find a partner who
equals you. There are
nine mix-n-match categories: small, medium
and big love bits, lust and lasting power. The
perfect matches are listed below. Hint:
The size of animal clues you in
to the category size.

HIM	HER
Horse	Elephant
Bull	Mare
Hare	Deer

If you're not a natural fit, don't make the bed and walk away. There's a position for every mismatch:

✽ A **deer-woman** can make the most of her small space by using the **Widening** (opening her legs as widely as possible), the **Yawning** (doing Widening but also raising her thighs) or the **Indra** (starting with Yawning, then bending her legs so her calves are against her bottom thighs).

✽ A **mare-woman** may tighten things up with the **Clasping** (you both keep your legs as straight as possible), the **Pressing** (as the name says, you press hard – but with the thighs as well as your groin), and the **Twining** (she twists one leg around his).

✽ An **elephant woman** can make like a mare while also clenching her legs together whenever possible to strengthen her *yoni*'s grip.

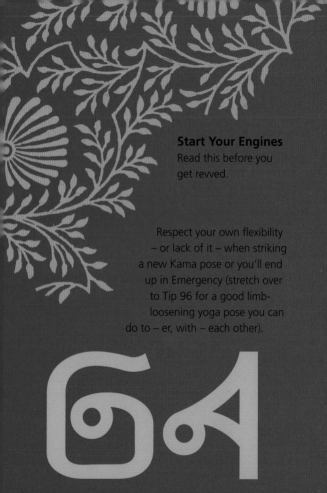

Start Your Engines
Read this before you get revved.

Respect your own flexibility – or lack of it – when striking a new Kama pose or you'll end up in Emergency (stretch over to Tip 96 for a good limb-loosening yoga pose you can do to – er, with – each other).

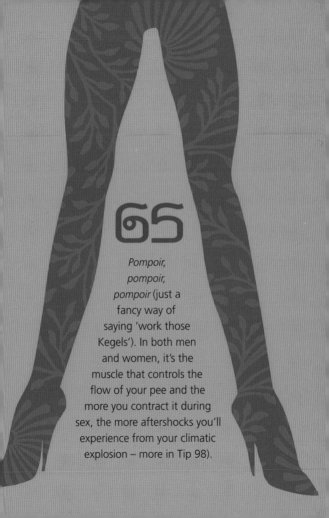

65

*Pompoir,
pompoir,
pompoir* (just a
fancy way of
saying 'work those
Kegels'). In both men
and women, it's the
muscle that controls the
flow of your pee and the
more you contract it during
sex, the more aftershocks you'll
experience from your climatic
explosion – more in Tip 98).

S-L-O-W down.
Nice and easy does
it every time. Three Kama ways to dawdle:

* **Halt jackhammering:** Rapid-fire
thrusting = lightning-quick finish. Rein
him in by grabbing his hips while he's on
top and directing him to decelerate. Or
roll on top so you're in working the gears.

* **Shake it up:** Tame the tempo by varying
positions. Slip and slide from Shiva (see
Tip 81) to Transverse (Tip 79) to Shakti
(Tip 78) and Transform Cow (Tip 80).

* **Pause between pumps:** A *yoni* is not an
oil drill – the more it's pumped at the
same power and pace, the less likely it
is to blow. Vary the speed and rhythm
of your old in-and-out – try going deep
a few times and follow up with a few
twisting shallow moves. Throw in a few
of the suggestions from the next tip and
watch out for the gusher.

The Kama Sutra is all about his-and-her pleasure. As such, it acknowledges there are a few things that every man, no matter how much of a super-*lingam* he has, will need to do during **Body Congress** to keep her *yoni* happy (especially if he's a fast shooter):

* **Move forward:** Pushing himself an inch or so up her body during standard Shiva (Missionary) makes it more likely he will include her clitoris in the love rubdown.
* **Churning:** The man moves back and forth in a straightforward manner. He holds his *lingam* in his hand and moves it around in her *yoni* as if stirring soup.
* **Piercing:** He penetrates her *yoni* from above then pushes his *lingam* against her clitoris.
* **Pressing:** He pushes hard… harder, harder!
* **Blow of the Boar:** He rubs both sides of her *yoni* with his *lingam* as he pulls in and out. **Sporting of the Sparrow** is moving the *lingam* rapidly and lightly in and out.

The Top 10

Given the national average of booty moments, even those who do it daily and twice on Sundays would need to invest over a year if they wanted to try every single one of the Kama Sutra positions. Because your days are probably already crunched, here are the Top 10 moves most guaranteed to electrify your play while still giving you time to revel in each other's presence. And the winners are…

Key:

N: These positions for newbies don't require much effort but there's no stint on payoff either.

M: Midwayers will get off on the challenge of mastering these slightly harder poses.

S: For Kama Sexperts only.

68

The Pestle
She lies with her legs parted wide and held out straight. He slowly enters her *yoni* straight on with his back slightly arched, working up some sparks by pressing his pelvic bone firmly against her love bump and rocking back and forth.
Best for: N
Make It Even Hotter: Slip a pillow under her bottom.

Splitting of the Bamboo

He kneels in front of her and she rests one of her legs on his  shoulder while leaving the other stretched out. She then alternates this position by switching legs.

Best for: M

Make It Even Hotter: She can stroke her bliss button while he does his stuff.

Pincers from the Front

He kneels, she sits on his lap with her legs either side of his hips and on the count of one, they both lean back supporting themselves on their hands. He stays absolutely still and she does all the thrusting.

Best for: N

Make It Even Hotter: She lies back and places her legs on his shoulders, holding onto his arms for support. They can ease into Open Pincer with him clasping her ankles and opening and closing her legs in time to her heave-hos.

71

The Ripe Mango Plum
She reclines and he kneels on one
leg by her side. Grasping her by
one leg, he gently pulls it back
over her head before inching
his way inside.
Best for: S
Make It Even Hotter:
The further he pushes
her leg, the more of a
head rush she gets
as the blood
rushes down.

Door Ajar

She kneels with one leg on the bed while standing on the other. He does the same behind her and then, holding her standing leg by the ankle, he lifts it up to his waist. She reaches behind and grabs his neck, while he holds her around the waist to keep them balanced.

Best for: M

Make It Even Hotter: She can reach down and diddle her own pearl deliciously with her free hand.

72.

Clasping

She straddles him and then slowly stretches out so that they are both lined up, limb-to-limb. They hold hands and squeeze together. To help them remain balanced, he keeps his feet flexed so that she can push against them with her toes.

Best for: N

Make It Even Hotter: She raises his arms out to his sides while lifting her upper body, pressing her groin against him even harder – like a snake ready to strike.

Twining

She lies on her side. He kneels behind her, facing in the direction of her head and slides his knee nearest to her between her legs. She should open her legs just enough to let him in.

Best for: S

Make It Even Hotter: Once he's in place, she can clamp her legs to work up that tight loving feeling.

Climbing the Tree

So called because it appears as though she is attempting to climb a tree, using his lingam as a strong branch to keep her from falling. Start by facing each other, standing. She lifts her leg (right or left, it doesn't matter) and balances it over his shoulder and slips him inside. Kiss, cuddle and run your hands all over each other.

Best for: S

Make It Even Hotter: With his help, she can lift her other leg so that he completely supports her.

Aphrodite's Delight

He catches hold of her feet so that her legs form a 'circle' and the soles of her feet are pressed against her sides (the higher, the better – the aim is for the soles of her feet to push against her breasts). Clasping her neck, he enters her.

Best for: M

Make It Even Hotter: She grasps her toes to increase the depth.

Wheel

He lies flat and she straddles him, lifting one leg and pressing her hands one after the other to slowly rotate around his *lingam* like a wheel.

Best for: S

Make It Even Hotter:
Nibble and kiss each new part of each other's body as it becomes accessible.

77

Hornier, Harder, Hotter

Even doing the Kama each time you come together can feel as if you're doing the old in-and-out after a while. Knock your knickers off with these scorching spins on the original.

In this **switcharoo on Shakti** (Woman on Top), he lies back and arches his back while pointing his property forward. She climbs on, facing her feet, and rear-ends him so that his goods stay bent down (careful he's not so pushed forward that breakage occurs!). The new angle of his dangle allows him to explore every inch of her inner sanctum, especially the oft-ignored sides, providing her with lusty sensations she didn't know existed.

78

Sweeten up the **Transverse** (classic Side to Side) with her lying stretched out on one side, one arm holding her head up. She raises her upper leg straight up. Once he hops aboard by straddling her lower leg, she can rest her raised leg on his shoulder. The unique angling gives this move a back-and-forth exhilarating edge over the regular up-and-down, over-and-out routine.

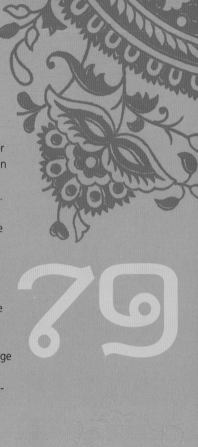

Transform Cow (Rear Entry) by having her kneel on all fours. He hits home from above, crosswise, as if he's doing a push-up over her body (if he keeps slipping out, he can slide into base from traditional Doggy and swirl sideways). To really rev up the stakes, he leans slightly backwards to take the whole of his weight on one hand and knee. To make her truly sit up and beg, he can move in tiny circular motions with his pelvis.

80

For **Shiva** (Missionary) with a sexy dollop of heat, she lies on her stomach and spreads her legs out slightly. He lies on top of her, and penetrates her from behind, vaginally or anally. She keeps things nice and tight by pressing her legs together (his legs are on the outside of hers). Once you're both comfy, twist around so that you're lying head-to-toe (he may have to turn sideways for a moment to pierce her *yoni*). Hold on to each other's ankles to stay connected.

Faster, Pussycat!

Just because the Kama is about otherworldly connections, this doesn't mean you can't get it on quickly when the passion between you becomes fever-pitch. These showstoppers will keep sync mind and body in sync:

82.

Driving the Nail Home

practically guides his hammer to her G-spot. She lies on her back and either brings her knees back towards her head or leaves them outstretched while he penetrates her from above. Once a nice steady rhythm is achieved, she pulls her legs back towards her head and he starts hitting to the hilt. Maintain your gaze throughout.

To get a **Rub Down**,
she lies on her back and
lifts her legs so that
they're over her ears
and parallel to the floor.
He kneels in front and, supporting her, presses
his upper body against her thighs so that he
joins her at the groin. Because her legs are raised,
her *yoni* is narrowed, so there'll be more show-
stopping shallow grinding against little-touched
nerves than simple head-on deep pounding.

She sits on his lap and starts
squirming him in to her like a
greased pole at a sex club. To get
into the beat, she moves and
grooves, wriggling her bottom,
squeezing her *yoni*, moving up and
down and all around. He can tip her
by reaching around and
letting his fingers do
all the walking over
her body, so they're
completely connected.

Wild Sex

According to the Kama Sutra, many of the moves we make during sex imitate animals. Get ready to unleash your inner beast (sound effects not included).

85

Crab Crawl

He lies on his back and then lifts himself up in a reverse push-up. She sits on his claw and then rotates to the right, placing her left leg under his right leg. She then brings up her other leg and rests the sole of one foot against his chest, leaning back on her hands. Don't expect to hold this one for more than a minute or two!

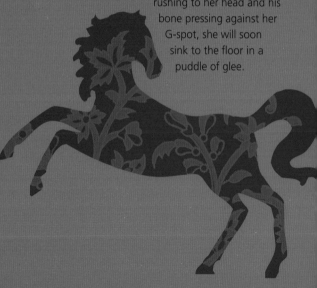

Gazelle and Stallion

He's kneeling and she wraps her legs around his waist and then, slipping his horn inside, she leans back until her head touches the ground. While she's holding onto his wrists for support and he's lifting her bottom, she raises her bottom up and slings her ankles over his shoulders. With all of the blood rushing to her head and his bone pressing against her G-spot, she will soon sink to the floor in a puddle of glee.

Blow of the Bull

Slip into Shiva (Missionary) but with him leaning out to her right, pulling her knees back up towards her face so that he's resting on the backs of her legs, penetrating her at a deep, deep angle that will make her tingle right down to the tips of her toes.

Dog
He mounts her from
behind, gripping
her waist. As they
bark it up, she
twists round
to gaze
at him.

Cat
She lies on her
stomach and he
seizes her ankles
with one hand, lifting
them high while reaching
with the other hand to tilt
her head back. Purr!

90

Bee
Any sweet move where she flits her honeytrap around his *lingam* to make them both buzz.

91

The Mare
When she forcibly holds him inside with her pelvic floor muscles and milks him dry.

Bliss

'When her passion has ebbed,
she should rest, bending forward to lay
her forehead upon yours
without disturbing your yoked bodies:
it won't be long before desire stirs again.'

Four words: Sex Heaven On Earth. What any hot-
blooded lover knows is that once you slow down and
really concentrate on every aspect of each other's
desires, it's nooky nirvana over and over again.
Because the real pleasure of sex isn't in the ultimate
thar-they-blow orgasm; it lies in making the magic last.

For too-hot-to-handle thrills that also keep you
bonded body and soul, add these scorching secrets
to your sensual line-up.

The Big Om

Sure, sex is the practice of life, not a pleasure performance – but why not practise to add more omigod to your orgasms?

Lock eyes during orgasm.
It's much harder to do than it sounds but its an amazing way to trip the light fantastic, adding a huge level of intimacy to your love bond.

92

93

The tendency is to hold your breath when the big moment comes. Instead, **try a huge exhale**, letting it all flow out.

Don't stop until you're both there (quick, jump ahead to Tips 97 to 99). Kama is fair in love and sex by stating that only once both parties have reached their climaxes can the party come to a close.

94

He should have a lot of tricks up his sleeve (refresh his memory and his *lingam* with Tip 67) – plus a **vibrator in his pocket**. As the Kama Sutra states, 'If a man is unable to satisfy a … woman, he should have recourse to various means to excite her passion'.

Practise yoga together. It will help you both limber up so you can twist your body into any pretzel position – it also improves your staying power and gets you more in sync with your lover. Ten minutes a day is all you need to transform yourself into a love guru: One of you bends over with feet and hands flat on the floor so your body forms an upside-down V. The other straddles the bender's back calves and, wrapping a strap around their waist, leans back. The bender walks their hands forward to push the stretch. Hold for ten breaths, then switch positions and repeat.

Kama Again

And again and again, with your guide to an ecstasy encore.

It's easy for her to keep the joy flowing – as long as he doesn't work to rule. Provided he keeps applying pressure in all the right places, her happy hour will never end. He can build the energy by varying the intensity – mixing in a little foreplay, some cuddling, back to foreplay, intercourse, more foreplay and so on.

Teach him to multiply. Working his pubococcygeal muscles (take a peek at Tip 65 for how to pump it up) will allow him control of his own destiny by teaching him how to orgasm without ejaculating. Once he can pump it up for a minute straight, he'll be able to clench his muscles at the crucial moment so he gets all the pleasure without losing his special wood-stiffening juices.

Three quick ways she can help hold back his lava flow while keeping his boy happy and hard:
* Change positions mid-game
* Stop and let him diddle her
* Grab his base.

Pillow Talk

The Kama Sutra stresses that it is extremely impolite to fall asleep too soon after sex. Some of the most intimate and passionate moments can happen during this time when you're feeling happy and relaxed. Here's what the text suggests you do instead:

100

Hose down. Although you may want to skip the honey and liquorice and just stick with some **fragrant bath oils**. Follow up with a rubdown.

101

Smooch and snuggle to savour the feel of each other's bodies and possibly 'rekindle love' (aka 'sex').

102

Whisper sweet nothings.

103

Have a post-love snack – the suggested menu is mangos, cold meats or sweets. Dagwood sandwich, anyone?

104

Head outside and stargaze.

105

Now go back
to Tip 1!

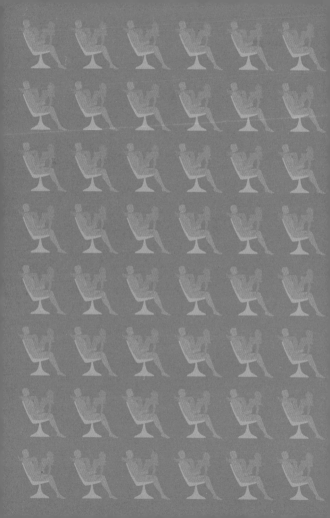